Rolling

A Ladies' Guide to Brazilian Jiu Jitsu

MELANIE FARMER

BURROW PRESS | ORLANDO, FL

© Melanie Farmer, 2023
Illustrations: Amy Wheaton
Book & Cover Design: Ryan Rivas
ISBN: 978-1-941681-24-4
POD edition. All rights reserved.
published by Burrow Press
burrowpress.com

"A wise and wry take on identity formation, parental expectations, and proper martial arts attire. Following a young woman's journey from student to teacher, this thoughtful essay's nimble voice provides a lively exploration of family bonds and the search for self-mastery."

Colson Whitehead

author of *The Nickel Boys*

IS THIS GUIDE FOR YOU?

As you hold this guidebook in your hands, you may be thinking, *Is this guide for me? What is Brazilian jiu jitsu? Will it suit me? You may also wonder, What skills do I have?* Or, perhaps you are concerned because you see yourself as unathletic, or even untalented generally. You may have tried other sports or hobbies in the past only to fail miserably. Maybe you have an array of hobbies and lack the follow through to commit to any one of them fully. You may simply have too much going on in your life right now to concentrate on something so trite and non-utilitarian as the study of a martial art.

Do not rush to make a decision just yet. There is much to explore. This book will gently guide you through these and other nagging questions that might hold you back from embarking upon the practice of ground fighting. As you reserve your judgement, put away concerns about your eligibility, agility, or aptitude. This book will address all these concerns and more while equipping you with the tools you need to assess your own potential as a practitioner of Brazilian jiu jitsu.

Let us begin with some visualization: Imagine the whole world has been waiting for you and cannot wait to hear what you have to say. Imagine you are powerful, impressive even. Imagine what you could be and then, moments later, imagine you are already that thing. Were the world a simpler place, this imagining might be enough. But since it is not, be prepared to work a little harder.

YOU ARE HERE

Brazilian jiu jitsu has the ability to empower and confuse. Through practice, and the advice of this guide, you will move from confused to empowered, but be warned: those around you may simply remain confused. A desire to have others understand your choice of sport will be an ongoing, ever-evolving want.

following an ambitious, failed attempt at an elusive career in another city, you move back into your parents' home. Though at the time it is a societal trend among people your age—brought on by economics, optimistic liberal arts educations, and foolish, learned idealism—knowing you are not alone does not lessen your shame. Hours spent staring at the slow-unfurling southbound asphalt of I-95 allows ample time for a sense of uselessness and regret to well up in your chest. Everything you own fits inside your 1999 Toyota Camry. In the driveway of your childhood home, your parents help unpack the car and welcome you back into the house to which you never intended to return.[1]

Your mother has replaced the furnishings in your bedroom with new ones that appear too big for the space. You feel a strange comradery with these inanimate objects because of this shared trait. At night, you sit on your bed and look for jobs the way you once slogged through last-minute essays for English class. Being in this room, typing as you are, reminds you that things are less simple now. You realize, perhaps crushingly, that you have no idea how to proceed. The job postings are littered with jargon you cannot decipher and you wonder if perhaps this is all a game. Or a series of riddles. Or maybe serious stuff that feels like a riddle—like the unlearnable exploded arrangements of lines and capital letters from your high school chemistry homework that once made you weep. You scroll through fonts, searching for one to give your resume panache—like you used to have. You fluff up descriptions of your minimal work achievements in jaunty columns and bulleted lists. You hope to one day render yourself useful again to the world.

---

[1] Outside of holidays and trips of five days or fewer

MAKING SPACE

One of the first lessons of Brazilian jiu jitsu is to remain calm. The key is to focus on what you can do rather than what you cannot. The game will teach you that, while on the ground, if your hips are held down it is likely that your torso is free. So, sit up. When grappling, the player on the bottom must create space for safety. Create a frame with your arms to protect your head and neck. While this space alone will not win you the match, it can help you stall for time until you figure out what to do next. Remember, even when you are on the bottom there are still options. Do not obsess about the moves you cannot make. Look for the ones that are open.

temporarily resigned to life in your parents' home, you begin to look for ways to get out. Even a few hours away from the place itself can potentially remind you that you are an adult in the world. You think of the things you would be doing if you lived elsewhere. After a brief google search for jiu jitsu gyms in the proximity of your parents' home, you discover one is extremely nearby, nestled in a strip mall between an Arby's and a Goodwill donation drop-off center. You have driven by this place countless times without even noticing it.

You started to learn to grapple when you lived in that other city—a hobby you wandered into in a why-not response to an invitation from a friend. The first time you tried it, you did nothing more than get held down. But you watched others move men twice their size. You witnessed the miraculous reversal of a small player sweeping another and ending up on top. You were absorbed by the strange calm of the game, its lack of impact and emphasis on flow. You did not understand how it was done, but you wanted to. You watched and tried and watched and tried, each evening when you stopped in at the gym. By day, you wandered the city and worked odd jobs. You wondered about how you could afford the rent on your basement room without the job you'd been released from. You read books on the metro and worked the pastry counter at a popular restaurant where everybody else that worked there was as young and aimless as you. You taught yoga to little kids who could not find their center of gravity. You collected paychecks in small bites. They added up to just less than what you needed.

But at the gym, nobody asked you about these things. At the gym, people showed you how to sweep, how to grapple. These things could be learned in a conversation. They could be repeated, right then, until you got them right. Grappling, unlike life, felt learnable. Making the little jobs work, adding up the paychecks not blowing them on cabs home from the dark bar in the middle of the night—these problems are not learned quickly or mastered through repetition. In the end, you resigned to them—your first tap out. You acknowledged the loss and got going.

So, when you sign up for the new gym, you do not have any real skill. With all that has happened, you barely remember what you once knew about the sport. But you remember the peace it brought you. The way it asked your brain to tinker. You wonder if that is still available to you here. The mechanics of the game. The mysterious methods of fighting on the ground. The pacing and flow. Its movements are a language you want to speak. In the wake of so many other discarded beginnings, you figure you can start to learn something new again.

You take the trial class. The people are friendly, and they assume you mean well. They assume you are listening. That you can learn. The coaches look at you as if they are surprised, not that you showed up, but that you stayed. They make eye contact and remember your name. They do not ask what you do for a living.

You sign up for a monthly membership. When you arrive back at your mother's house, you tell her you have been to the gym, knowing that she assumes you mean the YMCA up the street. When she asks, "Do you still have a membership?" you mumble, "Yes," and it is not exactly a lie.

OPPONENTS

Matches in Brazilian jiu jitsu are paired by weight and rank. In practice, however, it may not be possible to create an ideal match up. Not to worry: the game is constructed for the smaller player to win. Even when grappling with a stronger opponent, there is still much you can do and, with enough skill, you can even prevail. This is also true beyond the mat.

The ultimate opponent for a lady-practitioner of Brazilian jiu jitsu is most likely her mother. The looming, powerful presence of the mother figure in your life might render you a complete coward. It is likely you have already fought more imagined battles with your mother than physical ones with anyone. Even when equipped with the best training, she will remain your most challenging opponent.

you cover your bruises when you dress for your grandmother's ninety-fifth birthday party. By this time, your training habit is written all over your body in the form of tiny blood vessels pressed too hard and broken beneath the skin where they have leaked into circular shapes and jewel-toned colors. Alone in your childhood bedroom, you stand at the mirror and examine these little welts on your body. They are bright red, and deep blue, and regal, transitional purple. You like them. They are proof of the work you have put in and that you are not too weak for it. You consider short sleeves so you can wear them with the pride of a teenager boasting a freshly won hickey. They are the same kind of evidence, proof that you are grown up and that you know something now—something secret.

Despite your personal enjoyment of these little trophies, you must maintain an awareness that social custom demands something different of a lady. For this festive occasion, you select an outfit that strategically covers these proofs of your athleticism . It is crucial that the skirt grazes your knees and the boots completely clear your calves. Add a blazer.

When your mother asks about the bruises shaped like the hands of large men[2], she sees them because they accidentally peek out from the hem of your dress—a sign that you have yet to master the art of their concealment. When she asks, "What's that?" she is looking at you slantwise from the passenger seat over her left shoulder, an angle that triggers your muscle memory for being scolded. She does not want to hear how you got them, but she cannot keep herself from asking.

"Are those from that fighting stuff again?"

"Don't worry about it."

"Well, I should be worried about who's beating up on my daughter."

"That's not what it is."

"Then what is it?"

Riding in the backseat of your parents' car makes you feel like a child again, and this trip is one you made often when you were one. This conversation is also familiar, and you know that if you turn your head to look out the window, it will end.

---

[2] Because that's what they are

JUSTIFICATION

Your choice to become a martial artist will not sit well with your mother. It will confuse and cause her to fear for your safety. She will preliminarily cringe when she asks questions about what you do at the gym, even though you will only answer them in scraps. There will be a fragility to her emotions when she asks about this thing you do that she does not understand. She will ask questions that your honest answers may not satisfy. Navigating her confusion and disappointment will be another skill you build alongside your more athletic endeavors. Your coaches will train your body, but this battle is of the mind, and it is one you must undertake without their guidance.

after a few months in your mother's home, you settle into a pattern. By day, you slog through a fruitless job hunt. In the evening, you eat dinner at the table with your parents like you did when you were a kid—shouting out incorrect answers to Jeopardy questions between bites. After dinner, you put your plate in the dishwasher and head to the gym.

There, nobody knows what they want to be when they grow up. Many of your teammates are literal teenagers, trapped in what they think is the misery of tenth grade. Some people you meet seem as lost as you are—between jobs, relationships, and plans for the future. For some, this gym is the plan, and you can see the allure. It is a pleasant distraction, a world with simple, organized rules that govern it: keep your nails clipped, your equipment clean, no shoes, bow before you walk onto the mat.

To strangers who do not know what you do in any detail, your participation in fight sports means you are tough, and the men who train with you are assumed to be both confident and intimidating. It occurs to you how helpful this misconception must be for these men, your teammates. And you also wonder how to harness the mistaken assumption of your own confidence. If you can practice what it feels like to find success here, perhaps you can learn its mechanics, understand it on a level that gives you control over success itself. You know yoga people who are into "manifesting." They like to talk about "creating possibility," a bunch of hooey that you do not buy into, but the idea that you might be able to make a thing happen, any thing, sounds like it might be what you need right now. The thought is both foreign and familiar, like maybe you once believed it.

After the gym, you return home each night, shower, and strategically hide your sweaty gi in the corner of your bedroom. You maintain that your parental home is a only pit stop, unpacking partially so it is clear that you do not plan to stay. At night, you try to sleep in the room that used to feel like it was yours. You wonder about the dubious height of the bed your mother has purchased. You wonder if it is just in your mind that it seems much closer, closer than is safe, to the whirring ceiling fan. All the too-big furniture pushing you out, closer either to the ceiling or the door. It seems you can only escape or get chopped up.

EQUIPMENT

Fashion is an important undertaking for any lady, and a lady of Brazilian jiu jitsu is no exception. One can roll in a variety of types of athletic wear, but if you want to be a serious martial artist, you will need to purchase a gi. This garment is both clothing and equipment. It is a weapon that you wear.

USER NOTE: Due to the heaviness of its fabric, the weight of a gi soaked in the washer has the potential to aggressively accelerate the force of a washer's spin cycle. As a beginner, you may not realize this and may, at your own peril, wash your gi in your mother's washer without changing the spin cycle to low. Should this event result in the demise of an already decrepit appliance, be warned that the incident will be blamed on you entirely and, by extension, your "weird little gym outfit." Avoid this unpleasant scenario by keeping the spin cycle on low and only doing laundry on days when your mother is out of the house.

When you begin shopping for a gi, you are already aware that it has a specific, practical purpose that demands it be hard in places and malleable in others. It must be durable enough not to rip when your opponent pulls on it in the course of a roll. It must also be loose enough to be grabbed at the knees, shoulders, and lapels. It needs stiff collars and thick-weave fabric. Still, because it is a piece of clothing, it lives in the realm of fashion. And this is where the problems begin.

The makers of these garments are faceless to you but, in shopping, you learn that they are mostly straight men without girlfriends. You can tell by their vast misunderstanding of what appeals to the female eye. Pale lavender and all shades of pink, as if you're a little girl unaware of how to find yourself in this whole gender conundrum. However, as an adult woman, you have long been confidently able to assert your femininity without wearing pastels. The gi-designing men have not figured that out.

They begin by taking a completely fine and functional gi, then assaulting the garment with an array of embroidered flowers and butterfly-shaped patches to entice you into ownership. For you, these embellishments have the opposite effect. You spend hours scouring the internet in search of something more straightforward, regulation color, and in your actual size.

As your search goes on, you discover another unfortunate misunderstanding held by the girlfriendless straight men designing gis the world over: they think you need to be sexy while you roll. These men hire busty, luxurious females who appear to know nothing about the sport to don the uniform and pose for photos akin to those in a Sports Illustrated: Swimsuit Edition or Playboy centerfold spread. There are tits. They are oiled and gleaming and they rise up behind the stiff, practical collars of the product for sale[3]. In some cases, the poor woman has lost her pants. In others, she has not only lost her pants, she is not even modeling a women's gi—it is a men's gi, and her wearing it makes it look cool. Or something. She is likely also wearing a tauntingly visible thong[4].

None of this helps you, though. You are here for practical reasons. If you are lucky, you can get something in a regulation color that comes with pants. Because you wear pants.

---

[3] In case you forgot you're trying to buy a piece of athletic equipment here

[4] Since she can't find her pants

PHYSIQUE

As a female human in the United States of America, one of the greatest things you can be is skinny. You might also think there is some value in being kind or smart, but if you want to get anywhere in life, you should really put some thought and action into the whole being skinny thing. It unlocks a lot of doors.

Your mother barely tipped the scale at a hundred pounds on the day she got married, so she understands the social value of being skinny. She likely wishes a similar physique upon you, her progeny, for the sake of the many perks a thin life can offer. Still, such details of our bodily fates are out of human hands. You must make do with what nature provides. When you were little, your mother used to call you "pleasingly plump," which you mistakenly took as a compliment because you thought she was saying "pleasing me plum," which sounded all-around great.

That's not what she was saying.

Once you become a consistent jiu jitsu practitioner, you reap some of the standard rewards of any regular exercise routine, including: growing confidence, increased dopamine and serotonin levels, and, the most coveted result, weight loss. Though you are not waif-type skinny, your body takes on a fitter look that is inevitable when you sweat through thick layers of pearl-weave fabric daily and use your abs a lot. Your mother does not recognize the distinction between this and the coveted waif silhouette.[5] She is not interested in your skinniness as it relates to your level of newfound athletic accomplishment. She simply revels in the fact that it has finally happened to you, the least likely person to achieve the elusive greatness of being a smaller size than you used to be. She celebrates your smallness loudly, publicly, in front of friends, relatives, strangers, and in excess. In fact, her excitement about you being skinny may eclipse all your other life achievements.

She asks you: "What size is that dress?"

You answer, quickly and quietly, in hopes this particular line of questioning will end.

But she also asks: "And what size did you used to wear?"

And it seems she wants to go on in this way, like a never-ending vaudeville comedy routine.

When you consider her enthusiasm and pride, you wonder how long you can keep up with this new, smaller body. You will later learn that this body you've made is only temporary—the product of the shock to your system caused by so much fighting on the ground. Later, you will regret the loss of this momentary truce between you, your mother, and your sport. Mostly you will regret losing how close you came to having her see jiu jitsu as essential.

---

[5] If that's what you're hoping for, you should probably quit now

FEMININITY

If your mother is the kind of woman who always remembers to curl her hair, she likely spent a significant amount of time, skill, and dedication making sure you were clean, dressed, braided, decorated, dusted off, polished, re-polished, and properly presented during your youth. And, if you are the kind of woman who keeps her hair in a perennial messy bun, you may carry a simmering fear that you have, and always will, fall short of her expectations. Rather than try to be something you are not, consider embracing the fact that you are different from your mother. Perhaps it could be a point of conversation, a novelty even. Try making jokes about it. Or, consider occasional compliance with her desire for you to look more put-together. Your ability to play both sides will be a key source of your power.

One day, when you finally know enough to teach it, you lead a little one-time, jiu jitsu beginners workshop—just the basics. Since this feels like an accomplishment, you invite your mother out of some kind of childhood habit. It is an empty invitation. You are certain she will not show up.

You do not notice her when she enters, quietly, sliding in at the back of the room. When you do see she's there, you say hello and try to orient her, unsure if this is what she wants. She waves you off, suggesting you turn your attention to the other participants. The generosity of her don't-worry-about-me gesture is instantly mangled by your mind into something more like I-don't-want-to-be-here, which is what you'd assumed about her all along.

For the duration of class, she remains in the corner. She wears workout gear that is more fashion than function. Her hair is curled. She follows along with a wobbling uncertainty that you interpret as defiance. When she gets confused, you hesitate to help since, you think, she is something other than a student here—a spy or a judge or a decoy. You regret your accidentally invited uninvited guest.

As you talk to the people who want to learn, you see her fumbling out of the corner of your eye. You suspect she has come here solely to ignore your cues. You look away when she starts to slow down and, when she finally sits back on her heels, eyes on the ceiling, you have what you are waiting for. You wish she had just picked up and left instead of performing her idleness here so publicly, but you know she likes to keep her disapproval in context. She waves and smiles as she leaves the class or maybe, you can't remember, she gives you a quick and tiny hug as she heads out the door.

Later, at dinner, you hear her tell your father with excitement about all the things his daughter can do. She talks about the muscles in your arms and your knowledge and ability, your command over the room. She tells it like a kid who just came home from a marvelous field trip. Her eyes shine in just that way.

You wonder how she noticed all that while she was looking at the ceiling.

NAVIGATION

Brazilian jiu jitsu is a reactive game. It is sometimes compared to a chess match. It is a measured practice, one that is, at least partially, about pacing. You will learn to move when your opponent moves. As a beginner, it is hard to understand how to navigate an opponent. How to do more than attack to overcome them. You must learn to move with their movement. When you do, the game goes more smoothly. There is a beauty to this measured and specific timing.

Beginners exert too much energy, push too much, breathe too shallowly, move too quickly, apply more force than is necessary, and end up exhausted. This use of force and power must be replaced with patience and strategy. This will take time and practice.

As you start to learn the game, you will realize it is about placement and leverage. Timing and physics. You will start to see that you should not move forward until you know where you are headed, that you must let go of one grip if you are to establish another, that even the most well-planned submission might fail, and that the only way to handle that failure is to move on to something new. But you cannot move without first letting go.

In matches there will be two bodies imposing force on each other, but there will also be spaces, little holes that appear behind arms and beneath torsos. These passageways are there if you know where to look for them, but they are not static. They move when your partner moves. First you learn to find them, then to anticipate them. Eventually, you learn to find the places to put your feet like hooks, the morphing tunnels in the space under an arm that you can dive through, and where the fabric of the gi gathers like a handle that you can use to pull yourself into a better position. When explaining the dynamics of how to move, your coaches will tell you that it is easier to move around the mountain than to lift it. Remember this.

COMPANIONSHIP

While you do not go to the gym to meet men, there will be men there. Simply because they are your teammates, they will take on a too-close familiarity to you, like a gaggle of older and younger brothers that you never had. They will not interest you as dating prospects at all. Your mother may experience a heightened sense of concern and urgency when it becomes clear that your interest in jiu jitsu is not a passing phase. She may fear that the sport has the ability to permanently erode your femininity, thus decreasing your desirability in the dating sphere. Her desire to prevent permanent damage could result in increased interference in this area of your life.

When you are not at the gym, your mother stresses the importance of wearing skirts and makeup, going so far as to buy these items for you to assure you have enough in supply to properly assert your beauty. This is a concern of hers that is heightened by your perennial disarray, your male-skewed friend group, and your complete lack of dating interest in the lot of them. While she cannot control your actions, she peppers you with suggestions for how to make yourself more appealing.

She encourages you to develop at least a passing interest in a real, mainstream, American sport like football, despite your expressed distaste for it.

"Everyone likes football," she says.

"I don't."

"You just need to try harder. Do you want me to explain it to you?"

"Nope."

"Everybody needs to know how to at least talk about football."

"Not everyone likes football."

"They do."

You don't.

Luckily, at this point you have moved out of her house and so will not be forced to endure watching actual football games. This approved sport is surprisingly violent for your mother's tastes, but this is best left unmentioned. If she knew any details about your sport, jiu jitsu would likely concern your mother beyond its lack of mainstream popularity and weak potential for charming conversational content. She is unaware of all the time you spend straddling men's chests and squeezing their necks between your thighs. Holding men down and choking them with your biceps is hardly the ladylike behavior she seeks to engender in you. Luckily, her dim comprehension of what you actually do does not come close to this level of detail. You have come to believe that maybe it is better for her never to know.

"What's jiu jitsu?" she asks, again, like it's the first time.

"It's in the Olympics."[6]

This reply both verifies its legitimacy as a sport and guarantees she will never figure out what the sport actually entails. The execution of this brilliant, one-line shutdown is a sign of your increasing ability to move around the mountain. The less she knows about what you are up to, the less you have to explain.

---

[6] It's not

COMPETITION

When you think that you know enough, and with the encouragement of your coaches, you may feel compelled to sign up for a competitive tournament. You will sign up for the women's division and (mistakenly) believe this is a comfort. Instead, for the first time, you will reckon with your skills outside of the context of your tiny gym. The women you compete against will likely outrank you. They will be heavier and more skilled than you. Although you have trained in a pit full of great big men and learned to hold your own against opponents twice your size, as a first-time tournament-goer, you are really a featherlight novice.

When you arrive at the tournament site to weigh in, there is a dearth of female competitors. Suddenly, you are all lumped into a single group without divisions for weight or skill. You watch your male teammates weigh in across the huge gymnasium. They will go up against men their exact size and build, their skills carefully paired to ensure competitive matches.

At your mat, you are alone. Competition is the first time you become aware of how lonely it is to grapple: you versus a stranger. It adds to the feeling that you are untethered—to your team, your coach, your knowledge. And, once the round begins, your own body.

This is the moment you realize how embarrassingly little you know, how much there is to know, and how especially screwed you are for not knowing all of it right now. Even in this controlled environment, you learn that a fight is chaos. Game or no game, your body responds as if it is fighting off death itself. But even though it feels like a genuine threat to your life, it is (as you used to be able to remember) sport. There is a crowd here and ref and a clock and a lot of expectation. You trained for this. You should know how to do it.

You don't.

TAPPING OUT

Though it is one of the natural outcomes of competition, losing may not be top of mind for the enthusiastic beginner. After all, each match does not end with a loss, but rather, a tap. A tap is a voluntary exit. Taps are performed by the hand, firmly and definitively on any part of the opponent's body. If the hands are occupied, a clearly stated oral declaration of the word "tap" will achieve the same result. Loud noises made mid-match, if distressing enough, will be interpreted by refs as a verbal tap. Once called, a match ends immediately.

at your first competition, you discover new ways of being tired that you never knew about. You learn that you can barely stand chaos and yelling. Under stress, you are incapable of performing techniques that you have drilled in practice for months. Despite this, you also learn that you are less afraid of pain than you realized. You find you possess a strange, dormant determination, even in the face of your melting skills. You learn, and are surprised, that you do not have to talk yourself into coming back to the mat even after tapping again and again. You are tougher than you knew. You almost start to believe that you are different than you feel, like a legend about someone you have not met.

On the way home, you are overwhelmed by an expansive loneliness that you did not expect to feel today. Alone in your car on a familiar street, the silence seems to spread out in all directions, and you want nothing more than to talk to someone about what today was.

There is no one for this.

You stop at an IHOP and eat pancakes in the middle of the night and realize that only now, three hours later, you are coming down from the adrenaline. Your shaking hands fill your mouth with the sugar and carbs that you have not had in weeks. They taste unfamiliar instead of comforting like you had hoped. You take a huge headache and a half stack of pancakes in a Styrofoam box back to your apartment. All your muscles hurt. The empty feeling follows you into your apartment and fills the place. You lie in bed alone and feel your heartbeat in your throat.

RESETTING

After competition you will know yourself better as a player. What follows is a critical moment where you must decide what to do next. For some, the stress of competition may teach you that this is not the sport for you and that the best course of action is to move on to another, safer and less complicated hobby.

However, once you have mastered a technique, you no longer need to talk through it in your head step by step. You will deploy it without thought. You will find you are so good at moving around the mountain that you can anticipate the best route before it materializes.

When your mother enters your car on a hot afternoon there is junk on the passenger seat, and as she complains about your poor housekeeping, even though a car is not a house, she removes clothes and empty water bottles from the passenger seat so she can sit. When she unearths your gi where it has been strewn across the seat, she steps away from it and the car, gazing in and waiting for something to correct itself. You are aware that the something she waits on might be you.

As she lowers herself into the passenger seat, you have already moved your gi to the back seat. You will already have anticipated the question itself, and not just the question, but the way she inflects it and the fact that there is no answer that can satisfy it.

"So, you still do that fighting stuff?"

You won't respond.

ASSESSMENT

We started the journey through this guide by addressing the looming questions that may have pestered you as you began your practice. It is notable that few, if any, of these doubts will ever go away completely. However, as you once may have fled in the face of an opponent, you now know how to maintain your base, establish grips, and form a plan. Stay technical, attack, but remain calm. Most importantly, by now you have established the essential skill of developing ways to adjust your plan. Adjustment is the game.

You now have the training to begin with care, to take your time and move methodically. Let us conclude with a higher-level visualization, something you can take with you: Imagine that you are reaching forward. Establish a grip. Be prepared for your opponent to successfully slide that grip off. Reposition. Envision your new position. Reach again. Grip again. Feel the grip slide away. Reach. Lose. Grip again. Repeat. Adjust. Repeat.

ACKNOWLEDGEMENTS

Deep gratitude to the following lovely groups and people who made this chapbook possible:

Ryan Rivas for being an amazing steward of Orlando writing and for all the hard work of Burrow Press staff, in particular the Stetson University students who assisted in the editing of the chapbook: Xanthippe Pack-Brown, Kelly Liu, and Calista Headrick. Also, Amy for the skill, care, and attention to detail she put into these illustrations.

The Hurston/Wright Foundation for their celebration of this essay and their unrelenting support for Black writing and writers at all stages of their careers.

The faculty of the University of Central Florida MFA program especially Terry, Chrissy, and Jocelyn.

AWP and my writer-to-writer mentor Lara Lillibridge.

My beloved writing family of Longleaf Writers Conference and to other conferences that have welcomed me into the fold, inspired me, and kept me working.

To all my grappling instructors over the years going back to the very beginning, and all my BJJ gym friends, especially those at American Top Team.

To the friends who help me navigate life, writing, and procrastination, especially Amanda, Michelle, Dyannah, Tim, and Eric.

My family.

And finally, thanks to the readers.

ABOUT THE AUTHOR

Melanie Farmer is a Central Florida writer and educator who holds an MFA in Creative Writing from the University of Central Florida. She is the winner of a 2019 Intro Journals Award in creative nonficiton from the Association of Writers and Writing Programs and is the first winner of the Hurston/Wright Foundation's Crossover Award in literary nonfiction. Her work can be found in *The Tampa Review* and *Split Lip Magazine*.

ABOUT THE ARTIST

Amy Wheaton is an illustrator and graphic designer in Orlando, Florida. Find more of her work on the covers of Autofocus Books and at amywheaton.com.

CPSIA information can be obtained
at www.ICGtesting.com
Printed in the USA
BVHW012113110523
664021BV00016B/201